Fifty Favorite Poems
Federico Garcia Lorca
imagined into english by r soos

Cholla Needles Press
Joshua Tree, CA

sources:

obras completas. Madrid, Aguilar 1954
obras completas. Madrid, Akal 1980
obras completas. Galaxia Gutenberg 1997

http://www.chollaneedles.com

ISBN: 1979806128
ISBN-13: 978-1979806121

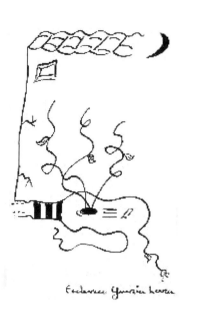

Federico Garcia Lorca (1898 – 1936) wrote poetry full of love, childhood, nature, death, ecology, painters, paintings, poets, and music. He uses irony, everyday language, and surreal language to express the images of the life he wishes to share with us. He uses and expands traditional forms of poetry to keep us grounded in history and current in our personal understanding of life. Lorca is an inspiration for all who live their life desiring creativity. His poems whisper, shout, laugh, cry, howl, and dance. His poems will make you want to whisper, shout, laugh, cry, howl, and dance.

sitting

I contemplate time
the heavens alone
portray silence

a white silence
circling with true strength
over my meditation

the purest light
colliding with dark numbers
between the stars

Federico Garcia Lorca

meditation beginning and end

time is the color of night
of a quiet night

with enormous moons
of eternity

stuck at twelve o'clock
having fell asleep forever

in her tower

the clocks cheat us
time has already passed

her horizons

one… two… and three

the hour rings out in this jungle
the silence is filled with bubbles

a golden pendulum back and forth
swings my face through the air

the hour chimes throughout the jungle
in the pockets of people

people walking back and forth
like groups of insects

I listened instead to my heart sounding
like my grandmother's gilded clock

indecision

she was caught
wavering near branches
caught in the breeze

the branches wavering
with her wandering thought

her small mirror reflects
the glow from her forehead
brought on by daylight

the light wavering
with the wandering branches

in darkness she wandered lost
dew falling from her eyes
captive of time wandering

as she wavers through branches
in the wavering starlight

the setting of this song
(Adolf in 1921)

after everything . . .

(the moon opens her golden tail)

… nothing…

(the moon closes her silver tail)

from the deep
a star falls as a peacock
from the sky

Federico Garcia Lorca

sunrise

the climax of dawn appears
the white crown of a golden rooster

the climax of my laughter appears
the golden crown of a rooster's shadow

all in all

the hand of the wind
caresses the deep heavens
over and over again

the stars blind our eyes
and our eyelids blink open
again and again

county fair

under the tuba sun
there parade passes

sighing with decorated
ancient captive horses

the fair
is a wheel

a wheel of light
through the night

the merry-go-round music circles
weaving in the air up to the moon

and there, there's the child
that all the poets forget

and a music box
playing in the breeze

jungle

I entered the forest of clocks
stalks swing tick tock
hourly clusters of tolling bells
unseen constellations overhead

black lilies
for the dead hours
and black lilies
for the newborn hours

all the same!
and what of golden love?

there is only one hour
only one hour!

the frozen hour

spiral

I will leave you here
with a lily in your hand
lover of my night

young widow under stars
I have encountered your truths
my tamer of night

you train the shadows of butterflies
as I leave walking backwards watching
with love always for a thousand years
and I see you watching me leave again
knowing I will return to hold you close

lover of my night
you train the shadows of stars
as I leave you here

on this dark blue path
you fill all my universe
you fit all my heart

west

in this exquisite sky
beyond the deep blue violence
are clouds torn like gray camellias

wishing for wings of freedom
escaping over the cold ridges

this sunset colored with deep shadows
prepares my soul for an immense night
without spirits or clear paths

the time of sphinx caterpillars

in your great garden
we flowers open our face
to these evil stars

we are born under
their horns - they crawl and devour
as we die slowly

¡this frozen time!
lyrical caterpillars
build mausoleums

and sit on our blue
mangled petals growing wings
and new confinement

Pan

How insane!

Pan's goat horns
have turned into wings

and like a great butterfly
he flies through forest fires

How insane!

lumberjack

walking in the twilight
they asked where I am off to
"out to hunt bright stars"

and while the hills slept
I came back with all the stars
in my old backpack

¡I chopped down and packed
all the white light of the night
in my old backpack!

hunter

¡above the pines!

four doves soar through the air

four doves fly and turn
with wounds washing away
their four shadows

¡below the pines!

four doves are on the earth

they chopped down three trees
for Ernesto Halffter

there were three
(the day came with its axes)

there were two
(silver tips on the ground)

there was one

there are none

(they left the water naked and alone)

trees (1919)

trees!

were you once arrows
now fallen from the blue?

what terrible warriors shot you?
did they come from the stars?

your music contains the souls of birds
your perfect passion comes
from the eyes of God

trees!

will the warriors ever know?
your rough roots have found
my heart in the earth

whims of fancy

sun

sun—who called you 'sun'?
nobody would be surprised
to see three letters

in the sky instead
of your bold golden face

pirouette

if the alphabet died
everything would die
words are wings

our entire life
depends
upon four letters

tree

tree
the e gives you leaves

moon
the oo gives you color

love
the l gives you kisses

Three Sunsets
for Conchita, my sister

I

the afternoon is full
of sorrow because he dreams
with noon (of red trees

and clouds over hills)
the afternoon loosened its
lyrical green hair

and trembles sweetly
… it is annoyed to be late
having once been noon

II

the afternoon starts now!

why? why?

… right now
I see the day incline like a lily
(the flower of the morning
bends its stalk)

… right now
the root of afternoon
rises up from the dark

III

goodbye, sun!
okay, I know you are the moon,
but I will not tell anyone, sun

you conceal yourself
behind the curtain
and make up your face
with rice powder

in daylight you are
the guitar of a farmer
at night you are
the mandolin of a clown

there is no difference!

your illusion is creating
a multicolored garden

¡goodbye, sun!
do not forget those who love you

the snail,
the old woman on the balcony,
and me...

I play with my spinning toy with my. . .
heart.

he died as the sun rose

night of four moons
and a lone tree
with one lonely shadow
and one perching bird

I search my skin for
a trace of his lips
the source kissing the wind
without touching it

I hold the No he gave me
in the palm of my hand
like a nearly white
lemon made of wax

night of four moons
and a lone tree -
at the point of a needle
is my love ¡spinning!

Federico Garcia Lorca

serenade
for Lope de Vega

by the riverbank
this night is being baptized
and near Lolita's bare breasts
the flowers die from love

the flowers die from love

night sings in the nude
covered by the bridges of Spring
Lolita lathers her body
with river water and perfume

the flowers die from love

the night is spice and silver
shining on the rooftops
silver from creeks and mirrors
spice from her white thighs

the flowers die from love

song of november and april

clouds in the sky
fix my eyes on white

to give them life
I bring them a yellow flower

I can't hold them still
they move on wandering and white

(between my shoulders flies
my soul, gold and satisfied)

the april sky
fixes my eyes on indigo

to give it a soul
I bring it a white rose

I can't inspire
white into the indigo

(between my shoulders flies
my tranquil soul, bold and blind)

water, where are you going?

I'm laughing as I follow the river
to the shores of the sea

sea, where are you going?

I'm going up river to search for
for a fountain and relax

and you, cottonwood, what will you do?

I don't want to say anything
I. . .tremble!

What I wish for, what don't I wish for
from the river and from the sea?

(Four birds without plans
remain in the tall cottonwood)

half moon

the moon moves across the water
how can the sky remain so sober?

slowly the moon cuts through
the ancient quivers on the river

while a young frog
uses her as a mirror

Federico Garcia Lorca

horizon

on a green haze
a rayless sun sets

shadows on the shore
dream alongside a boat

and the close proximity
leaves a melancholy spirit

in my aging soul
a small silver pulse echoes

what would I give
to find a kiss from you?

a kiss that wandered
from your lips to mine
might kill me with love!

(my lips will taste
the earth of a shadow)

what would I give
to gaze deep into your dark eyes?

auras of radiance swell
and display the face of God!

(stars blinded my eyes
one morning in May)

and what would I give
to kiss your chaste thighs?

(primordial rose crystal
sediment of sun)

first anniversary

she lives in my frontal lobe
oh, what an ancient truth

what is the use, I wonder
of ink, paper and poems

to me your skin appears
as red lilies and soft reeds

dark haired love in the full moon
how much do you crave my passion?

second anniversary

the moon stabs the sea
with a long horn of light

gray and green unicorn
shaking with ecstasy

the sky floats on the air
like a giant lotus flower

(oh, you alone walking
through our home last night!)

Debussy

my shadow becomes silence
near the water of the channel

in my shadow are frogs
hidden from the stars

the shadow brings my body
reflections of quiet things

my shadow becomes a
giant violet insect

a hundred crickets look bronze
with light through the bulrushes

the light is born in my chest
reflecting from the ditch

the awesome presence

I want water to wander beyond riverbeds
I want wind to travel beyond valleys

I want night to see without eyes
and my heart to be without a golden flower

I want the oxen to converse with giant leaves
and the earthworm to die alone in shadows

I want teeth in the skull to be bright
and yellows to flood through silk

I can see the anguish of the wounded night
wrestling with desire for noon time

I can endure a poison-green sunset
and the broken arches of suffering time

but please do not reveal your smooth body
like dark cactus exposed among the reeds

leave me with desire for your dark planets
and do not show me your youthful waist

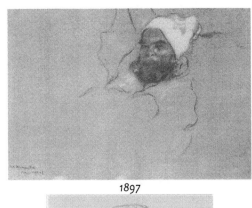

1897

1898

1918

Three portraits of Paul Verlaine by William Rothenstein

Three Portraits with Shadow

Verlaine

the song
I will never sing
has fallen asleep on my lips
the song I will never sing

there was a firefly
on the honeysuckle
and the moon poked
the water with lightening

and then I dreamed
the song I will never sing
the song full of lips
and distant rivers

the song full of hours
lost in shadows
song of a star living
through an eternal day

Federico Garcia Lorca

late afternoon

was that my Lucía with her feet in the
stream?
three giant cottonwoods and one star

the silence diminished by the frogs
sounds like gauze painted with little green
moons

a dry tree by the river
has flowered in concentric circles

leaning over the water I dreamed
of the dark haired girl from Granada

the truth

ah, how hard it is
to love you as I love you

for your love
the air pains me
and my heart
and my hat

who would buy
this hatband from me
and this sad of white thread
I use to sew handkerchiefs

ah, how hard it is
to love you as I love you

the guitar

my guitar begins to cry
the hearts of sunrise shatter
the guitar begins to cry
don't waste time hushing her
it's impossible to quiet her
she cries alone with songs of
how the water cries
how the wind cries
over fallen snow
it's impossible to quiet her
she cries for distant things
hot deserts in the south
which beg for white camellias
she cries for arrows which miss their target
the afternoons with no tomorrows
and the first dead bird from the nest

O guitar
heart badly wounded
by five unearthed truths

and afterwards
the chaos
who created time
vanishes

(only the desert remains)

the heart
source of desire
vanishes

(only the desert remains)

the illusion of kissing
you as the sun rises
vanishes

only the desert remains
- the undulating desert

six strings

the guitar
makes dreams cry

the cry of lost souls
escape through her round mouth

and like the tarantula it weaves
a great star to catch the sighs

that float in her dark
wooden reservoir

dance in Seville

Carmen is dancing through the streets
with her white hair and glittering pupils

girls - close the curtains!

a yellow snake coils on her head
as she dreams of past lovers in her dance

girls - close the curtains!

the streets are empty and the shadows
predict
bitter hearts are out searching for old thorns

girls - close the curtains!

sudden love

no one understood the perfume
of dark magnolia hidden in your womb
no one knew how you tortured
a hummingbird of love with your teeth

a thousand persian ponies sleep
in the moonlit plaza of your brow
while for four nights I kept my arms
around your waist to stay warm in snow

in the midst of plaster and jasmine
your eyes were a pale garland of seeds
I searched through my heart to give you
perfect ivory poems that say always

always, always, garden of my grief
your body forever running from me
the blood of your veins fills my mouth
your mouth is dark with my death

memory of love

don't take your memory with you
leave it here alone in my heart

a white cherry tree trembling
in this tormented January

a wall of bad dreams
separates me from the dead

I give the pain of a fresh lily
to a heart of new gesso

all night in the garden
my eyes are like two dogs

all night I am eating
venom filled light

at times the wind
is a fearful tulip

a sickly tulip
in the winter sunrise

I'm separated from the dead by
a wall of bad dreams

quietly the grass covers
the gray valleys of your body

near the rainbow where we met
hemlock is growing

please leave me your memory
leave it here alone in my heart

wailing

I've closed my balcony
because I don't want to hear the wailing

but beyond the gray walls
all that is heard is wailing

there are too few angels that sing
there are too few dogs that howl

many violins fit in the palm of my hand

but the wailing is an enormous dog
the wailing is an enormous angel

the wailing is an enormous violin
the tears have muzzle the wind

and all that is heard is weeping

Federico Garcia Lorca

woman lying in the sun

seeing you naked I think of the earth
a smooth earth untrampled by horses

a pure earth without weeds or blemish
a pure body everlasting on a silver horizon

seeing you naked I understand the longing
of the rain that seeks for a delicate waist

or the feverish ocean with an enormous face
which discovers no glow on its lonely cheeks

blood will sing out the bedrooms
and will rise with flashing swords

where the toad's and violet's hearts are
-you will never know where they are hid

your womb is a tangle of roots
your lips a dawn without a horizon

beneath your bed's warm roses
dead men moan and await their turn

the rose

the rose wasn't looking for the dawn
almost eternal on its stem
it was looking for something else

the rose wasn't after knowledge or shadows
the confines of flesh or dreams
it was looking for something else

the rose wasn't looking for the rose
poised stoically against the sky
it was looking for something else

absent soul

neither bull nor the fig tree know you
nor the horses nor the ants in your house
neither does the child or afternoon know you
because you have died forever

neither the spine of the stone
nor the black satin in which you lie know you
your secret memories don't know you
because you have died forever

autumn will come with seashells
grapes fog grown and gathered in hills
and no one will want to look in your eyes
because you have died forever

because you have died forever
like all the other dead on this earth
like all the dead who lie forgotten
in a fenced off heap like silenced dogs

no one knows you, no, but I sing for you

I sing for your profile and your grace
the dignified maturity of your knowledge
your craving for death and flavor of its mouth
and the sadness your valiant joy possessed

a long time will pass before another
like you is born - if ever he is born -
so lucidly distinct and so rich in adventure
I sing of your elegance with weeping words

I remember a sad wind through olive trees

sweet lament

I'm afraid of losing the wonder
of your stony eyes and the accent
that lulls me to sleep at night with
the lonely rose of your breath

I'm saddened to be here on this shore
a tree with no branches and I'm sorry
for the most is having no flower or clay
or pulp for the worm of my suffering

if you are my secret treasure
if you are my cross and my tears
if I am the dog of your kingdom

do not let me lose what I have won
and allow me to trim your river
with my lunatic leaves of autumn

wounds of love

this light, this devouring fire
this gray landscape around me
this ache of focusing on one ideal
this torment of heaven, earth and time

this cry of blood which decorates
my pulseless guitar lubricates
this weight of the sea pounding in me
this scorpion that dwells in my heart

this garland of love, this bed of wounds
where without sleep I dream of you
within the ruins of my sinking heart

and though I seek the peaks of reason
give me your prudent heart while I lie down
with hemlock and the spoiled passion of
science

the poet speaks truth

I want to cry out my pain and tell you
so you'll love me and cry for me
in a twilight full of nightingales
a dagger and kisses and you

I want to kill the only witness
to the assassination of my flowers
and turn my tears and my sweat
into an eternal mound of hard wheat

do not allow this confusion to ever end
the I-love-you and you-love-me that burns
under a worn out sun and old moon

may what you don't give and I don't ask for
be all for a death which does not even leave
a shadow for our trembling desires

love sleeps in the poet's heart

you'll never understand how I love you
because you sleep in me and you are asleep

weeping I hide you, haunted
by the voice of a piercing knife

standards which shake both flesh and spirit
have already entered my aching heart

and turbulent words have bitten
the wings of your severe spirit

people leap through the gardens
waiting for your body and my agony
on shining horses with green manes

but stay asleep my love my life
hear my chastened blood through the violins

look, they continue to glare at us in judgment

the dark doves

for Claudio Guillén

through the laurel tree branches
I saw two dark doves

one was the sun
and one the moon

my neighbors, I called
where is my grave?

in my tail said the sun
in my throat said the moon

and I continued strolling
along the waist of the earth

and saw two snow eagles
and a naked girl

one was the other
and the girl was neither

little eagles, I called
where is my grave?

in my tail said the sun
in my throat said the moon

through the laurel tree branches
I saw two naked doves

one was the other
and both were neither

statement

when I die
bury me beneath the sand
with my guitar

when I die bury me
among the orange trees
and the mint

When I die
bury me, if you desire,
on a weathervane

but wait till I die!

from here

tell my friends
that I have died

water always sings
under the fluttering forest

tell my friends
that I have died

(how the cottonwoods
with such silky sound!)

tell them I stayed here
with my eyes wide open

and that my face is covered
with immortal blue handkerchief

oh!

and that I went without bread
to my heavenly body

Books by R Soos

In Bed And In The Bathtub (1970)
Why Poetry (1974)
My Homeland (1976)
Reality Is A Drunken Feeling (1978)
Patient Rains And Petals (1981)
A Foreign Landscape (1984)
His Power (1988)
Dried Blood (1990)
The Son is Breaking Through (1992)
Garden Songs (1995)
Each Day (1997)
California Breeze (1998)
Moaning & Groaning (1999)
Train of Love (2000)
Guitars (2001)
Fiddlin' Around (2003)
Insecurities (2005)
Bringing In The Sheets (2012)
Parting/Departing (2015)
Selected Poems 1965-2015 (2015)
Somersaults With Life (2016)
Cell Notebook (2017)

Instrumental Piano CDs by R Soos:
California Breeze CD
Bringing In The Sheets (Soundtrack)

all available at amazon.com/author/soos
stay up to date at rsoos.com

Other Books Published By Cholla Needles

r soos – Cholla Needles 2017 Yearbook
Cynthia Anderson – Waking Life
Zara Kand – Interiors
Zara Kand – Exteriors
Noreen Lawlor – Sacred Possibilities
Noreen Lawlor – Tangled Limbs And Prayers
Cindy Rinne – Moon of Many Petals
Rees Nielsen – That's What I Painted
Robert DeLoyd – Upon Ashen Roads
Jean-Paul Garnier – In Iudicio
Susan Abbott – Nasty Woman Rise
Michael Dwayne Smith – Roadside Epiphanies
James Marvelle – Lasting Notes
Ram Krishna Singh – God Too Awaits Light
r soos – Cell Notebook
Steve Braff – 40 Days
Connetta Jean – Picture A Haiku

http://www.chollaneedles.com

Available locally at Rainbow Stew Gifts in Yucca
Valley, Space Cowboy Books in Joshua Tree, and
Raven's Book Shoppe in 29 Palms.

Available worldwide at Amazon.com

You will also enjoy our monthly literary magazine,
Cholla Needles – along with our monthly readings
at Space Cowboy Books. Thank you for reading!

18827456R00037

Printed in Great Britain
by Amazon